GAMING AI

GAMING AI

WHY AI CAN'T THINK
BUT CAN TRANSFORM JOBS

GEORGE GILDER

SEATTLE   DISCOVERY INSTITUTE PRESS   2020

Description

Pointing to the triumph of artificial intelligence over unaided humans in everything from games such as chess and Go to vital tasks such as protein folding and securities trading, many experts uphold the theory of a "singularity." This is the trigger point when human history ends and artificial intelligence prevails in an exponential cascade of self-replicating machines rocketing toward godlike supremacy in the universe. *Gaming AI* suggests that this belief is both dumb and self-defeating. Displaying a profound and crippling case of professional amnesia, the computer science establishment shows an ignorance of the most important findings of its own science, from Kurt Gödel's "incompleteness" to Alan Turing's "oracle" to Claude Shannon's "entropy." Dabbling in quantum machines, these believers in machine transcendence defy the deepest findings of quantum theory. Claiming to create minds, they are clinically "out of their minds." Despite the quasi-religious pretensions of techno-elites nobly saving the planet from their own devices, their faith in a techno-utopian singularity is a serious threat to real progress. An industry utterly dependent on human minds will not prosper by obsoleting both their customers and their creators. *Gaming AI* calls for a remedial immersion in the industry's own heroic history and an understanding of the actual science of their own human minds.

Library Cataloging Data

Gaming AI: Why AI Can't Think but Can Transform Jobs
by George Gilder—64 pages
Library of Congress Control Number: 2020947220
Paperback ISBN: 978-1-936599-87-5
EPUB ISBN: 978-1-936599-88-2
Kindle ISBN: 978-1-936599-89-9
BISAC: COM004000 COMPUTERS / Artificial Intelligence / General
BISAC: COM031000 COMPUTERS / Information Theory
BISAC: BUS070030   BUSINESS & ECONOMICS / Industries / Computers & Information Technology

Publisher Information

Discovery Institute Press, 208 Columbia Street, Seattle, WA 98104
Internet: http://www.discoveryinstitutepress.com/
Published in the United States of America on acid-free paper.
First Edition, October 2020.

THE BRADLEY CENTER

Gaming AI is sponsored by the Walter Bradley Center for Natural and Artificial Intelligence at Discovery Institute. The mission of the Bradley Center is to explore the benefits as well as the challenges raised by artificial intelligence (AI) in light of the enduring truth of human exceptionalism.

The *Walter Bradley* Center for
NATURAL & ARTIFICIAL
INTELLIGENCE

Visit us at CenterforIntelligence.org and MindMattersNews.com.

CONTENTS

INTRODUCTION:
FROM POINT GO

"Mesmerized by my quest to create machines that thought like people, I had turned into a person that thought like a machine."
—KAI FU LEE IN *AI SUPERPOWERS*, 2018

ARTIFICIAL INTELLIGENCE HAS BECOME THIS EPOCH'S PRIME BATTLE-ground in technology, philosophy, and even religion. At stake is a new demotion of the human race. Deeming the human brain a sub-optimal product of random evolution—a mere "meat machine"—the new computer science relegates human minds to a level below computer brains, and sees no limit to the ongoing ascent of machines and the corresponding descent of humans.

Pivotal to this conflict is a new take on the ancient game of Go. Invented in China some four thousand years ago, Go is a challenge of logical thinking that exceeds chess in its strategic intricacies and degrees of freedom. Offering 2×10^{170} (2 times 10 to the 170th)—essentially limitless—possible positions, Go began as a rigorous rite of passage for Chinese gentlemen and diplomats, testing their intellectual skills and strategic prowess. Later, crossing the Sea of Japan, Go enthralled the Shogunate, which brought it into the Japanese Imperial Court and made it a national cult.

A game of territorial control and maneuver, Go provides a stringent test of human minds in combat. It begins with an unoccupied board with a 19 by 19 grid of lines, providing 361 points of intersection. On these "points," one player positions black stones and one player white stones, resulting in elaborate geometries across the board. The player who surrounds and captures the most territory wins.

Players must anticipate both the moves of their opponents and the interrelationships between positions. These patterns represent reflexivity—the circular relationship between cause and effect—as contestants constantly assess and reassess the possible outcomes of moves and countermoves.

This ancient game became a template for the new fashion of Agent Based Modeling (ABM), in which computers simulate (and predict) the dynamic interactions of individual agents. ABM avoids the loss of information inherent in averaging, randomization, and statistically based modeling. It has been used to map traffic patterns, ecological interactions, financial crises, market movements, and other emergent phenomena. Go is almost a pure expression of such interactive dynamics.

With Go, AI got personal. In Seoul in 2016, Lee Sedol, a thirty-three-year-old Korean and the eighteen-time human champion of Go, played against AlphaGo, a program created by Google's DeepMind division. And Sedol lost.

How was this possible? Starting with the rules of Go and the goals of the game, the AI arrived at its strategies through a machine learning program. The essential technique is guess, measure the error, feed it back, and adjust the weights of the various inputs, until the output converges on an optimal winning solution. Modeled on a crude image of human brain processing, the computer learned from records of human expert moves, and by reinforcement through playing against itself. It parsed millions of previous games of Go for the crucial patterns of success and then deployed them to beat Sedol four times out of five.

More portentous still, in October 2017 Google's DeepMind launched AlphaGo Zero. This version was based solely on reinforcement learning, without direct human input beyond the rules of the game. In a form of "generic adversarial program," AlphaGo Zero vied against itself repeatedly billions of times. It became its own teacher. "Starting tabula rasa," a paper by the developers concludes, "our new program AlphaGo

Zero achieved superhuman performance, winning 100–0 against the previously published, champion-defeating AlphaGo."[1]

The program employed two key machine learning techniques. One, invented by Paul Werbos[2] and later popularized by D. B. Parker[3] and David Rumelhart, Geoffrey Hinton, and Ronald Williams,[4] is "back-propagation." Feeding back the errors, this method corrects the system by adjusting all the neural weights of its "neurons." The entire network adapts until the outputs conform to a pattern of targets—such as a winning position in Go. The second breakthrough is "genetic programming," developed and popularized by John Holland[5] and his doctoral student John Koza,[6] which "evolves" new techniques by competitive survival of the fittest.

In retrospect, AI skeptics like me disparage such feats as mere rote computer processing. If a program can make millions of moves a second, arriving at the right one seems routine. But none of us actually predicted it. In a game of logic and strategy, a machine learned how to defeat a world champion human by dint of computer pattern-recognition and feedback loops alone.

The feat was repeated in January 2019 with the complex video game StarCraft II, which offers more degrees of freedom even than Go. Iterating through data of inputs and results from half a million game records and performing some two hundred years' worth of games, the program arrived at an optimal strategy that prevailed against human champion contestants.

DeepMind cofounder Demis Hassebis expects such programs to outdo humans in many areas: "The reason we test ourselves and all these games," he says, is as "a very convenient proving ground for us to develop our algorithms [for uses in] the real world."[7] Prime early targets include diagnosing diseases, searching for vaccines, and preparing computerized tomography scans.

Indeed, why could not such a machine reproduce and excel all human industrial progress? Why could computers not parse the immense oceans of big data and learn all there is to learn? Why will computers not discover new laws of physics, cure cancer, create vast new wealth, and extend life?

Minds and Machines

PHILOSOPHERS AND ENGINEERS HAVE claimed that the human brain is essentially a machine ever since the great Gottfried Wilhelm Leibniz floated elegant analogies between engines of gears and cogs and the ganglia of human cognition. Arguing against a purely physical model of mind, he concluded that if the mechanisms of the human brain were expanded to the size of a giant building you could walk through, you would find cogs and gears but no thoughts.

Several hundred years later, Berkeley philosopher John Searle repeated the Leibniz logic with a famous analogy of the "Chinese Room." Searle imagined a clerk in a room receiving Chinese words from the outside and returning English translations according to a set of rote instructions. Searle pointed out that the clerk need not know anything about Chinese. A computer performing a similar function would not need to know any Chinese, either. In the sense of human conscious knowledge, a computer knows nothing at all.

Nonetheless, great scientists continued the pursuit of computer "minds." John von Neumann's last book, published in 1958, bore the title *The Computer and the Brain*. Full of insights, it implied that machines and brains have much in common. Ray Kurzweil's bestseller *How to Create a Mind* drew close analogies between mental processes and computer processors and predicted a "singularity" in 2041 when the processors would prevail.

These days AI programs digest press releases into news stories and compile data into academic tomes. AI has become the most fraught focus of international rivalry, the most coveted capstone of industrial progress, the most tempting new weapon of strategic power, the most fashionable model of mind, the most widely favored eschaton or "final thing." It becomes, in the words of novelist Neal Stephenson, an "entire system of the world"—a way of understanding the course and vector of technological fate, and thus the destiny of the human race.

In this epistemic shift, the Go breakthrough was pivotal. As the Chinese American titan Kai-Fu Lee explains in his bestseller *AI Super-powers*,[8] the riveting encounter between man and machine across the Go board had a powerful effect on Asian youth. Though mostly unnoticed in the United States, AlphaGo's 2016 defeat of Lee Sedol was avidly watched by 280 million Chinese, and Sedol's loss was a shattering experience. The Chinese saw DeepMind as an alien system defeating an Asian man in the epitome of an Asian game.

Moreover, the event and others like it, such as a 2017 confrontation between AlphaGo and a young Chinese Go champion named Ke Jie, inspired a crucial change. Lee, writing from Beijing's Zhongguancun neighborhood—known as China's Silicon Valley—called the defeat of Ke Jie China's "Sputnik moment," recalling the time the Soviet Union shocked the United States by launching the first satellite into orbit. According to Lee, the AlphaGo victory "lit a fire under the Chinese technology community that has been burning ever since." Less than two months after Ke Jie's defeat, the Chinese government launched an ambitious plan to lead the world in artificial intelligence by 2030. Within a year, Chinese venture capitalists had already surpassed US venture capitalists in AI funding.

Lee knows this subject well. He has held major jobs at Apple, Microsoft, Google, and now at Sinovation Partners back in China. He spearheaded the US entry into China on the wings of AI prowess, and he teaches AI to young Chinese entrepreneurs. Lee has transcended nationality to become a kind of digital diplomat from a new world of intelligent robotics and the Internet of Things, and in his opinion, the artificial intelligence successes with Go stand at the center of an inflection point in the history of the human relationship with technology: Go has launched an epochal narrative in which machines may well conquer the human mind.

More AI successes have quickly followed Go's. Two scientists at Carnegie Mellon, Tuomas Sandholm and Noam Brown, had been working for fifteen years on an AI poker player; in August 2019, they announced their success in *Science*. Their AI "Pluribus" program defeated an array of champion poker players under no-limit hold'em rules.

A supremely simple game focused on guesswork and bluffing, poker differs radically from Go. But the pattern-recognizing powers of Pluribus, based on its projective command of millions of previous and possible games, prevailed over the intuitive maneuvers and deceptions of poker players geared to outperform other humans. Once again, machines beat humans in what seemed to be a peculiarly human domain.

Then, toward the end of 2019, AI reached beyond portentous but ultimately trivial mastery of games to address one of the major scientific challenges of the era. AlphaGo became AlphaFold and pioneered a new standard in protein folding.

In the human body, the sixty-four codons of DNA can program cellular machines called ribosomes to create specific proteins out of the standard twenty amino acids. But the proteins cannot function until they are intricately folded in many plectic dimensions. Translating DNA codes into actual proteins—the words of the genome into the flesh of actual proteins—has become a major obstacle to the triumph of biotechnology. As the AlphaFold developers explain:

> Scientists have long been interested in determining the structures of proteins because a protein's form is thought to dictate its function. Once a protein's shape is understood, its role within the cell can be guessed at, and scientists can develop drugs that work with the protein's unique shape.

Over the past five decades, researchers have been able to determine shapes of proteins in labs using experimental techniques like cryo-electron microscopy, nuclear magnetic resonance and X-ray crystallography, but each method depends on a lot of trial and error, which can take years of work, and cost tens or hundreds of thousands of dollars per protein structure. This is why biologists are turning to AI methods as an alternative to this long and laborious process for difficult proteins. The ability to predict a protein's shape computationally from its genetic code alone—rather than determining it through costly experimentation—could help accelerate research.[9]

The industry conducts annual protein-folding competitions among molecular biologists around the world, and in 2019 DeepMind defeated all teams of relatively unaided human rivals. Advancing from the unaided human level of two or three correct protein configurations out of forty, DeepMind calculated some thirty-three correct solutions out of forty.

This spectacular advance opens the way to major biotech gains in custom-built protein molecules adapted to particular people with particular needs or diseases. It is the most significant biotech invention since the complementary CRISPR (Clustered Regularly Interspaced Short Palindromic Repeats) method for using enzymes directly to edit strands of DNA.

Because of such successes, many observers believe that Kurzweil's "singularity" is at hand, when machines will outperform human brains by every clearly definable standard. There is reason to believe, however, that AI is currently enjoying an Indian summer. The game of Go is a symbol of machine ascendancy; but in the course of time, scrutiny of such games will illuminate the real relationship between human brains and machine learning. In coming decades, it will become inexorably obvious that artificial intelligence is just the next step in computer science.

Yes, the field of AI will generate many useful devices. But its ambition to create computers that outperform human minds and are independent of human interpretation suggests a profound and crippling case of professional amnesia. The current generation of computer scientists has lost touch with the most important findings of their own profession. Dabbling in quantum machines, they defy the deepest findings of quantum theory. Claiming to create minds, they are clinically "out of their minds." Real intelligence is not a game.

The profession sorely needs an education in its own heroic history.

1. Beginnings at Bletchley Park

THE ASSOCIATION OF GO WITH AI IS NOT NEW. GO WAS AN INSPI-ration for the most important early accomplishment of AI.

At the outset of World War II, Bletchley Park north of London was the site of the first great practical breakthrough of artificial intelligence. Here the legendary computer titan Alan Turing led a team in creating special-purpose computers that exceeded all human capability in breaking cryptographic codes. Called "bombes," these computers hacked every successive version of the Enigma code used for German military communications, outperforming both the human intelligence of Nazi cryptographers and the human intelligence of unaided British codebreakers.

Later in the war, Turing led the design of a computer called Colossus, using over a thousand vacuum tubes. Colossus almost instantly cracked the codes used by the German High Command to communicate with one another. In the United States, a parallel effort concentrated on breaking the codes of the Japanese. In turning the tide in World War II, these "bombes" and Colossi pioneered by Turing may have been even more important than the atomic bombs of the Manhattan Project.

During his tour at Bletchley, Turing took time off to teach Go to his almost equally ingenious colleague I. J. ("Jack") Good. At the time, Go already seemed an ultimate game of pure strategy and trial of human intellect. Its mastery by Japanese adversaries suggested the study of the game as a route to insight into Japanese modes of thought. Turing and Good used the game as a way of sharpening their wits for the cryptographic challenge.

The success of Colossus encouraged dreams of ever-more-powerful computers and eventual general-purpose processors. While Turing predicted that machines would eventually conquer the more structured game of chess, the idea of a machine that could outperform humans in playing Go might have seemed formidable even to him.

In 1965, Good expounded more concisely than anyone before or after him the ultimate vision behind the movement to create AI:

> Let an ultra-intelligent machine be defined as a machine that can far surpass all the intellectual activities of any man however clever. Since the design of machines is one of those intellectual activities, an ultra-intelligent machine could design even better machines. There would unquestionably be an "intelligence explosion" and the intelligence of man would be left far behind. Thus the first ultra-intelligent machine is the last invention that man need ever make, provided that it is docile enough to tell us how to keep it under control.[1]

In the decades following the Good prophecy, AI enthusiasts predicted a coming planetary utility, a computer at once centralized and diffused, feeding on galactic floods of data and streams of energy to "think" and to replicate. Such a cosmic machine utterly dwarfs individual human brains confined to relatively tiny cranial cavities, bodies, and households.

To some, superhuman powers seem inevitable in machines that learn from volumes of data beyond any single human grasp, collect new data in oceanic streams beyond any mind, analyze it in massively parallel processors functioning at billions of cycles per second (gigahertz), and feed back the results adaptively to program fabrication systems or even factories.

Israeli historian Yuval Noah Harari epitomized this vision in his bestseller *Homo Deus*. It follows Karl Marx's inspiration, envisioning a new industrial revolution as a "final thing," an eschaton, obviating all human labor forevermore. But Harari bursts far beyond the meager horizons of Marx to declare that robots, genetics, cyborgian superhumans, self-driving transport, omniscient search and social networks, together comprise a transcendent artificial mind. Woven into an internet of all things, it will leave human beings with nothing to do but to pursue eternal life and pleasure as new forms of human gods, *homo deus*. But the "One Machine" engulfing the earth and invading the universe seems to be the new vessel of divine omnipotence.

Unlike Turing, Jack Good lived long. He died only seven years too soon to see the triumph of AlphaGo, which persuaded many observers of the truth of the Good prophecy in the Google age.

In reality, however, the new AI ascendancy is only the latest phase of the immemorial fantasy—from Laplace to Turing, from Faust to *The Matrix*—of thinking machines.

Following the Bletchley-born musings about computers that could replace human brains came Turing's American counterpart Claude Shannon, the inventor of the prevailing model of information theory in the years immediately after the war. Shannon's definition of information as surprise, or *entropy*, or unexpected bits, underlies all modern computer networks.

In a weak moment, though, Shannon speculated: "I think man is a machine of a very complex sort, different from a computer, i.e. different in organization. But it could be easily reproduced—it has about 10 billion nerve cells... and if you model each one of these with electronic equipment it will act like a human brain. If you take [chess master Bobby] Fischer's head and make a model of that, it would play like Fischer."[2] Turing, too, used to say of his machine, "I am building a brain."

Here we have what I have termed the "materialist superstition" of computer science. Computer theorists widely believe that the brain is nothing but a material processor, a "meat machine." Both neuroscientists and computer theorists claim mounting evidence for a purely physical brain.

The further message, anticipated by Good, is that keeping a machine mind under control is still an unsolvable problem. When a new supreme intelligence emerges, it is hard to see how an inferior human intelligence can govern it. As Elon Musk put it, "It's potentially more dangerous than nukes."[3] The late Stephen Hawking pronounced, "The development of full artificial intelligence could spell the end of the human race."[4]

Max Tegmark, MIT physicist and author of *Life 3.0*, explains why such an AI "breakout is almost inevitable." When humans came along, after all, the next-cleverest primate had a hard time. Subdued were virtually all animals; the lucky ones becoming pets, the unlucky... lunch.[5]

Although this vision of triumphant machines springs from experience with special purpose devices such as game machines, it depends on the idea of an *all-purpose problem solver*. Even an artificial intelligence compounded of multiple application-specific devices would require a general-purpose machine to integrate its functions, manage its priorities, and give it the capability of judgment.

The idea of a general-purpose processor springs from a particular set of assumptions about human minds and computers. The entire industry worships at the shrine of the Turing machine—the abstract mathematical computer conceived by Turing in 1936, which was so general in purpose that it could be programmed to execute any digital algorithm at all.

Consisting of a tape memory that passes back and forth under a programmable head that can change, erase, or rewrite a single digital bit on the tape at a time, the Turing mechanism is supremely simple. A step-by-step process of serial logic, it can process any problem, from arithmetic to tensor calculus, from word processing to image rendering. It provides a conceptual model for a general-purpose problem solver, which many computer scientists imagine is a reasonable definition of human intelligence.

By building a general model of a digital processor, Turing decisively advanced the abstract logic of computer science, making it possible to define what is theoretically "computable" and what is not. In an extension of Gödel's incompleteness theorem—where the axioms of a system cannot be proved within that system—Turing showed the limits of computation: All computers are dependent on outside programmers that he called "oracles." He wrote, "We shall not go any further into the nature of this oracle apart from saying that it cannot be a machine."[6]

Anything any computer can do, any algorithm, is executable on a Turing machine. Assembled in vast arrays and accelerated to ever-faster speeds, Turing machines become supercomputers deployed across global networks.

Importantly, for believers in computer supremacy, these machines are not restricted to digital operations. So-called "quantum computers" and other analog machines use real world primitives, inputs, and "superpositions" rather than only binary off-on codes. But they are still far from achieving proficiency. Digital Turing machines can be fed by sensors, meters, and imagers. The industry's increasingly powerful analog-to-digital converters could translate all phenomena—continuous analog waves of electricity, light, pressure, temperature, or sound—into Turing's digital language of bits and bytes.

Unifying electronics with a mathematical model of computation, Turing's thrust of abstract genius and generalization steadily gains momentum. Driving it ever forward is the continuing miniaturization of wires and switches under the Moore's Law pace of a doubling of computer power every eighteen months (as predicted by Gordon Moore in 1971). If some task eludes the machine this year—real-time translation of Mandarin into Urdu or instant Navier-Stokes fluid dynamics solutions; autonomous cars in a blizzard, virtual reality metaverses in your glasses or contact lenses, even optimal routes for traveling salesmen—the industry could just wait for the next Moore's Law bounty to be delivered in eighteen months or so.

Linking the Turing processors are what might be termed Turing networks—general-purpose worldwide webs of glass and air transmitting information at the speed of light. Fiber optics is the supreme embodiment, expanding its bandwidth year after year as the optical industry advances even faster than Moore's Law.

A corollary of the Turing-machine faith is the mantra "software is king." As the legendary venture capitalist Marc Andreessen famously put it, "Software eats everything." Hardware becomes merely an ever-faster and more compliant slave for the Silicon Valley oracles and visionaries, who tell the hardware what to do in a variety of software languages, these days mostly permutations of "C," Java, and Python.

Silicon Valley doesn't like paying for hardware—general-purpose step-and-fetch-it processors, which are dismissed as "plumbing." Interconnecting the processors around the globe should be "dumb networks," broadband networks neutral and accessible to all, Turing machines extended through general-purpose fiber optics.

In this regime, the best hardware is the simplest and most general-purpose, most closely approaching the Turing ideal. These are reduced instruction set computers—RISC machines—like the SPARC processors that Google's Eric Schmidt used to help design at Sun. Nearly all smartphones run on RISC machines, often designed and licensed by the British firm ARM (Advanced RISC Machines). Led by Huawei, many are moving toward the new RISC5 architecture from Berkeley with its open source code free to all to use. In the world of digital technology, RISC machines are as close as we come to the practical embodiment of abstract Turing machines.

2. Rapture of the Nerds?

WHAT COULD GO WRONG IN THESE LITURGIES OF TURING WORSHIP? What the Googlers and other exponents of software *über alles* sometimes seem to forget is *Turing's caveat*. Turing explicitly assumes *infinite* time and space, memory, and processing cycles. Turing even specified an infinitude of "printers' ink." Infinite things may prove a problem to procure.

In Silicon Valley, the onrush of Moore's Law and the nearness of Fry's Computer seemed to offer a suitable proxy for the needed infinities. After all, what do you want? Serial computers function at a clock rate of three to four billion cycles a second, tapping memories in the exabytes—10^{18} bytes. Could Turing even have imagined that? Forget printing and printers' ink. Think of a veritable infinity of screens. Infinity seems merely a shorthand for Silicon Valley's ever-expanding horizons of digital page-ranked abundance in sand and glass and air.

Infinity and ever-expanding horizons only exacerbate another problem with step-by-step serial processing, however. As von Neumann first recognized, serial processing faces a bottleneck: Different memory addresses always differ in distance from the processor. Called the "von Neumann bottleneck," or, today, the problem of "NUMA"—non-uniform memory access—it has never been resolved.

In response to the bottleneck, von Neumann proposed a massively parallel architecture called *cellular automata*, which led to his last book before his death at age fifty-seven. In *The Computer and the Brain*, he contemplated a parallel solution called neural networks, which were based on a primitive idea of how billions of neurons might work together in the human neural system.

Von Neumann concluded that the brain is a non-von Neumann machine nine orders of magnitude (a billion times) slower than the gigahertz he prophesied back in 1958 for computers. Amazingly, von Neumann anticipated the many-millionfold "Moore's Law" speedup that we have experienced.

But he also estimated that the brain is nine orders of magnitude (a billion times) more energy efficient than a computer. In the age of DeepMind and its rivals at Google, or Big Blue and Watson at IBM, the comparison remains relevant. When a supercomputer defeats a man in a game of chess or Go, the man is using twelve to fourteen watts of power, while the computer and its networks are tapping into the gigawatt clouds of Google data centers around the globe.

In the age of AI, Machine Learning, and Big Data, the von Neumann bottleneck has philosophical implications. The whole computer industry is von Neumann machines. The more knowledge that is put into a von Neumann machine, the bigger and more crowded is its memory, the farther away is its average data address, and the slower is its arrival at relevant real-time answers. Danny Hillis, MIT's visionary founder of the erstwhile Thinking Machines and author of *The Pattern on the Stone*,[1] writes, "This inefficiency remains no matter how fast we make the processor, because the length of the computation becomes dominated by the time required to move data between processor and memory."[2] That span, traveled in every step in the computation, is governed by the speed of light, which on a chip is around nine inches a nanosecond—a significant delay on chips that now bear as much as a thousand miles of tiny wires.

William Dally, a longtime colleague of Hillis at MIT, now chief scientist at NVIDIA, saw early in his career that the serial computer had reached the end of the line. Most computers (smartphones and tablets and laptops and even self-driving cars) are not plugged into the wall any more. Even supercomputers and data centers suffer from power constraints, manifested in the problems of cooling the machines, whether by giant fans and air conditioners or by sites near rivers or glaciers. As Urs Hölzle of Google comments, "By classic definitions, there is little 'work' produced by the datacenter" since most of the "energy is exclusively converted into heat."[3]

Living in the real world, we constantly run into intrinsically parallel problems. Consider images that flood the eye all at once or sounds that converge on the ear, whether you are following a tune at a concert or driving a car in the snow or summoning a metaverse with computer-generated graphics. The climax of all this parallelism is finding patterns through "machine learning" argosies across the seas of big data.

These naturally parallel phenomena call for a parallel computer architecture, where all the streams are processed simultaneously, rather than a serial channel processing bits and bytes one at a time. In recent years, parallel processors have been taking over the industry in the form of "graphics processors," which handle the simultaneous arrival of graphics pixels in an image.

The man who built the first crude graphics processor, the precursor of all of the industry's data center "neural networks," was Frank Rosenblatt, a psychology professor at Cornell. Modeled on mammalian brains, neural networks function at the system level, arraying transistors into networks of "neurons" inspired by the nodes of the human brain. As we know, the basic steps to the solution are *guess, measure the error, adjust the answer, feed it back* in a recursive loop.

In 1958 Rosenblatt described his "perceptron" to the *New Yorker*: "If a triangle is held up to the perceptron's eye, the association units connected with the 'eye' pick up the image of the triangle and convey it along a random succession of lines to the response units, where the image is registered.... [A]ll the connections leading to that response are strengthened"—i.e., their weights are increased in the pattern according to a process called "backpropagation." (The fanciful use of "eye" for *photosensor* did not stick, but a more fanciful name did: following von Neumann, the "response units" are now known as *neurons*.) As Rosenblatt prophetically concluded, "It can tell the difference between a dog and a cat."[4]

Four years later, Ray Kurzweil, then sixteen, visited Rosenblatt after Kurzweil's MIT mentor Marvin Minsky exposed serious limitations in the one-layer perceptron that Rosenblatt had built. Rosenblatt told Kurzweil that he could surmount these limitations by stacking perceptrons on top of one another in layers.[5]

Rosenblatt died in a boating accident on his forty-third birthday, never having built a multilayered machine. But by the twenty-first century Rosenblatt's perceptron was enshrined at the Smithsonian and his single-layered limitation was being remedied in computer science laboratories and industrial data centers everywhere.

Rosenblatt's view of multilayered recognizers prefigured machine learning. Learning is essentially the capacity to recognize patterns in data. The machine processes the pixels in tagged or identified images of your face hundreds or thousands of times. Then by comparative processes—in essence, superimposing images on top of each other and finding mathematical commonalities—it can flag new images of your face.

This pattern matching becomes even more useful when translated to different surroundings, such as a crowd at an airport. Moving up a ladder of abstraction as Rosenblatt recommended to Kurzweil, the machine can address higher-level abstractions, such as "terrorist threats" or police presence. With the availability of larger bodies of data, the range and accuracy increases.

In *How to Create a Mind*, Kurzweil lucidly explains the many layered process: A hierarchical machine learner will recognize letters at one level, words at another, phrases at another, and on up the scale to paragraphs and deeper meanings. Google calls its Go-mastering machine-learning division "Deep Learning." At some putative pinnacle, these multilayered devices can discover "new laws of physics" or limn the face of God.[6]

Complementing these software systems is ever-more-elaborate hardware—in recent years, data centers filled with parallel processors, often graphics chips linked by top-of-the-rack switches to other boards of parallel processors, and across the data center by fiber optic lines to other racks of computers, and then across cities, states, regions, and the world. The possibility of an integrated global computer system seems to be emerging, a system with access to nearly all the world's data, and with the capability of "understanding" that data and responding to changes in real time. Ultimately this machine could constitute a global operating system and adaptive control system for the world.

All this technology finally consists of wires and switches: communications lines branching at transistor crosspoints or "gates"—all those spangles across the electromagnetic expanse of the web.

Executing logic billions of times faster than human brains, these devices can be shaped as *transducers*, sensing sounds, brightnesses, frequencies, and pressures far beyond the capacities of eyes and ears and skin. Beyond the power of thought, these machines have led to new fabrication equipment such as 3D printers. These can translate the digital codes of AI into physical shapes and chemical reactions.

Such a cosmic computer is what has been called the ultimate "rapture of the nerds." Writers such as *Wired* co-founder Kevin Kelly celebrate their rapture by reciting the ever-mounting statistics of the internet: four billion phones, fifty billion "things," from sensors and antennas to cars and satellites, endless quadrillions of transistors, riding on oceans of data mounting beyond terabytes and petabytes and exabytes on into the mind-boggling zettabytes.

But for all its exalted claims, the AI "system of the world" (or "model of the multiverse," to use another phrase of Neal Stephenson's) finally rests on the more mundane engineering view of wires and switches. In pondering the question of whether wires and switches can think, we can gauge possible obstacles in this path to the trans-human future.

The exponential curve of Moore's Law has made the switches—the logic gates and sensors—relatively easy to build, and dirt cheap. The necessary complement to abundant switches is abundant wires, which brings us back to a major problem for AI. As Caltech engineer and physicist Carver Mead puts it, "In the end, everything gets choked off by the wires."[7]

Constraining every system is the reach and bandwidth of communications. If you cannot integrate the various intermediate results, synchronizing the processing steps, you cannot finish an intelligent process. The problem is that in every information system, the wires multiply by as much as the square of the number of nodes or transistors. Whether in brains as computer scientists understand them or in microprocessors as they make them, all intelligent processing is ultimately limited by connectivity.

Wires congest the silicon surfaces of chips and the dendritic wetware of the cortex of the brain and the backplanes of computers and the ganglia of eyes and the wiring closets of businesses and the ionic passages of the central nervous system and the under-street circuitry of giant cities.

Today wires constrain the newest internet security architecture and currency design, the "distributed ledger" of blockchains. This new "distributed" architecture entails broadcasting or "distributing" or "gossiping" the hash or mathematical summary of every incremental block of transactions on the chain to all the nodes of the network.

The glut of wires has bedeviled all the grand claims for centralized technologies since the mainframe computers at IBM and the giant central switches of AT&T. As wires increase by a power law with the increase of transistors and processors, nodes and neurons, wires eventually constrain computation.

The result is to compel *localized* solutions and distributed architectures. Machine intelligence faces the same constraints that force distribution of human intelligence. The human mind doesn't agglomerate in data centers. It is localized and dispersed in billions of minds around the globe. The new AI and machine learning movement is only the latest force to deny this reality.

3. Two Zettabyte "Connectomes"

Casting light on all these speculations about the nature and challenge of AI is the relatively new biological domain of "connectome" studies. If computers are networks of connected wires and switches, brains are networks of connected neurites (neural links of all kinds) and neurons (neural nodes).

Launched by Olaf Sporns and his team at Indiana University and popularized in the definitive *Connectome* by neuroscientist Sebastian Seung of MIT, connectomes originated in brain science. But computer and communications engineers will find this model familiar since it repeats in biology the connectivity schematics for both computers and networks of all sizes. In simple terms, a connectome is a detailed map of all the connections in a system.

If the connectome of the human brain is a map of all the links among all its neurons, the cybernetic connectome of human society might be a map of all the links across the internet.

Decades ago I offered an image of such transcendent interlinked computation as seen through a spectroscopic image of the internet from far in space. All the world's information is gravitating to the electromagnetic spectrum: enforced by the speed of light, the regularity of electromagnetic carriers makes possible the separation of contents from conduit at the end of the transmission. Mapping the mazes of electromagnetism in its path, an eye with a full-spectrum lens would see the web of computation as a single global efflorescence, a resonant sphere of light.

Capturing all the emanations of the world's computing and communications links, this image would be the physical expression of what now might be termed a "connectome." With each arc of electromagnetic radiation bearing a signatory wavelength, the luminous ball would reflect James Clerk Maxwell's universal rainbow, all governed by the speed of light.

As the mass of data traffic flows through fiber optic trunks, the skeleton glows in infrared, with backbones looming as focused beams of 1,550 nanometer radiance. With four billion teleputers or smartphones spread across the planet, engulfing the infrared skeleton is a penumbra of microwaves from 700 megahertz to five gigahertz, suffused with billions of pulsing sparks from three-gigahertz pods, pads, and palms. Spangling the penumbra are billions more nodes of concentrated standing waves, each an internet host with a microprocessor running at microwave frequencies also around three gigahertz.

They gather into pseudo-solar spheres of incandescence in data centers and reach up to satellites with cords of "light" between earth and sky in the Ku band between twelve and eighteen gigahertz. All these radiations are merging into an Internet of All Things encompassing everything from automobiles and drones to homes and offices in scintillating wavescapes that outline a galactic process of integrated computation.

As the intensity of the light rises—as every year a doubled flood of photons of traffic flash through the webs of glass and air—the change pushes up the overall frequency or average color of the light. Traffic on cable coax runs at radio frequencies in the hundreds of megahertz. The lasers of fiber optics cycle a million times faster than the oscillators in a conventional cable TV system. Moving into silica threads of fiber, the flow leaps upward in the spectrum to focus at 153 terahertz infrared. WiFi 5G signals and even WiFi 6 fibrillating from every pico antenna will rise into the sixty-gigahertz band, more than ten times the 4G level.

So as the brightness increases, its average color also inches up the spectrum. The global iridescence changes its dominant hues. If it were a rainbow, the center of intensity would move up from red through green toward violet. If it were a meteor, the Doppler blue shift of the internet would suggest that it is approaching you.

In the 2020s, Kevin Kelly of *Wired* consummates perhaps the grandest model of this transcendental computer. He projects the existing internet into a cornucopian future of four-dimensional artificial intelligence. The machine will gain a body, with every screen an eye and a portal to the AI cloud. Revived will be Yale computer scientist David Gelernter's *Mirror Worlds*, affording every physical point a digital four-dimensional vessel of augmented or virtual reality and artificial intelligence in time and space.

In Kelly's view of this virtual world of prosthetic programming and processing, our nervous system becomes an extension of the machine. It's at our Gatesian "fingertips" or haptic Google Maps or emerging neural taps. Thoughts summon things and master them in virtual forms. In the coming Internet of All Things, a procreative marriage of atoms and bits, the Web will own every bit, a black hole sucking everything into it. Humans become part of a single global agency. Kelly at various points dubs this global agency the "One Machine," "the Unity," or "the Organism." The new web is its operating system in virtual reality. As Kelly puts it, "The One is Us."[1] (Here, insidiously, returns the singularity.)

Kelly supposes that this cosmic computer will also provide an unimpeachable past (rather than a *1984*-style nightmare of ever-altered history) through cryptographic blockchains. Conceived in 2009 with the introduction of Bitcoin, the blockchain is a distributed immutable ledger of time-stamped facts and transactions. Beginning as a guarantor for money and transactions, a blockchain can certify facts, contracts, documents and accounts needed as a warrant of the veracity and security of the past. It would ensure against the nihilist vision of chaotic change eclipsing all memory and identity and language—and thus coherent thought, including artificial intelligence itself.

Listening to the computer scientists, you will be awed by the size of the connectome of the global computer system. Just to store all the details of connectivity of the global internet would take a map of links comprising a number of bytes on the order of zettabytes: 10 to the 21st bytes. That's a 1 with 21 zeroes after it, hard to even imagine. Total storage on the net reached the zettabyte level around 2017.

Let us pause and marvel at this humanly created connectome of wires and switches. It is indeed an immensity of connections. If the internet can really be integrated into one global system processing all global data, it will indeed outperform the unconnected and dispersed billions of human brains for many purposes.

Computer scientists normally stop with this reverent observation of the internet connectome. But the idea of connectomes began with brains, not with computers.

Only one biological connectome has been mapped in detail. That is the nervous system of a nematode, the millimeter-long roundworm *Caenorhabditis elegans*, which comprises 300 neurons linked by 7,000 connections. Defining this connectome took ten years. Engaged in nematode neural research for four decades, from the Nobel labs of Sydney Brenner to his own explorations at the University of Wisconsin, Anthony Stretton sardonically observed: "And knowing the connectome does not answer the question of how the nematode brain actually works. In many ways, I 'knew' more about the nematode brain when I started than I do now."[2]

This enigma of nematodes only intimates the far more baffling complexity of human brains. As MIT's Seung explains, "Your connectome is 100 billion times larger [than *C. elegans*], with a million times more connections than your genome has letters."[3]

To identify the features of the human connectome entails electron microscopy that can resolve many of the details of neuronal linkages.

Seung estimates that a single cubic millimeter of brain tissue yields a petabyte (10 to the 15 bytes) of image data, equivalent to a digital album of a billion slides. For comparison, the brain of a mouse bears a volume of about a thousand cubic millimeters. A human brain is about a factor of a thousand times as large as a mouse brain, adding up to a million cubic millimeters. Just registering the basic map of the human connectome thus will require a million petabytes of visual information. A million petabytes is 10 to the 21st, a zettabyte.

When you add up all these links, you arrive at a surprising conclusion: One human brain commands roughly as many connections as the entire internet. To map the connectome of a single human brain takes roughly the same order of zettabytes as to map the connections of the entire web.

Further, while the brain uses just fourteen watts to animate its zettabyte connectome, the zettabyte links of the internet connectome use hundreds of gigawatts, enough to power entire cities or countries. It may be surprising, but it's true: Computer networking and storage technology uses billions of times more energy than a single human brain, but is far less complex and multidimensional.

Why the difference? For one thing, the internet connectome is essentially founded on binary silicon and silica systems of Boolean logic and electronic and photonic processing, whereas the human connectome is embedded in multidimensional carbon and combines myriad electrical, chemical and even quantum interactions as well as photonic signals.

Even were we to conquer the problem of energy, enthusiasts for connectome studies must still face Stretton's paradox of connectome knowledge. Whether in the nervous system of a worm, in the weave of hardware and software of a computer, or in the ganglia, glia, synapses, dendrites and other wetware of a human brain, once you map all the links you still do not understand the messages or their meaning. Knowing the location and condition of every molecule in a computer will not reveal its contents or function unless you know the "source code."

The game of Go, touted as the launching point for AI's conquering of the human mind, is in fact an inexorable symbol of the futility of AI as an ultimate model of intelligence in the universe. The astronomical range of possibilities for positioning the stones is suggestive of the flaws of determinism. To you as an individual human player, it affords free will and choice. Yet in sheerly physical terms, you are just deploying patterns of smooth small white and black stones. All the symbolic freight of the saga of the game depends upon your role as interpreter of the meaning of the stones. With no interpretant, there is no strategy and no symbolic meaning. There is no winning or losing. There is no game.

As a technology, AI is hugely promising. As a system of the world, it offers no special insights beyond the steady advance, ever since Bletchley Park and World War II, of information technology. Modeled on the prevailing image of human brains as "neural networks," which in turn are modeled on schematics of computers, artificial intelligence is rooted in a grand circularity. Neural networks replicate brains assumed to be organized as neural networks.

4. Is Reality Binary?

THE FUNDAMENTAL PROBLEM OF THE AI VISION WAS EXPLAINED in the early twentieth century by philosopher Charles Sanders Peirce. In a critique of binary logic consisting of objects and their symbols, he showed that all mental activity is *triadic*. It comes in threes rather than twos. It connects objects and symbols through an *interpretant*. All software and hardware, mathematical models and projections, computational simulations and logical extrapolations, depend on *maps*: translations of physical entities into symbols. Maps consist of distillations of objects into representations of them.

The problem is that *the map is not the territory*. Whether in a mathematical equation or a mathematical model consisting of functions and equations, or in a neural network reflecting a sensorium of global measurements, AI supremacy assumes the essential identity of sufficiently refined maps and territories. AI is based on manipulating symbols as sufficient and reliable representations of their objects.

By asserting that there is always a gap between the object and the symbol, Peirce foreshadowed the coming of the AI emperor and his new clothes. Whether a number or a word or alphanumeric code or an analog report from a sensor, the symbol is always intrinsically different from the object it designates or describes.

Denying this cognitive and interpretive gap, the AI movement does not banish it. Instead the singularity movement simply explains it away. It correctly declares that any gap also afflicts human intelligence, and thus is irrelevant to a contest between humans and machines. The AI triumphalists assume that like two runners fleeing a grizzly bear, the artificial mind will prevail merely by exceeding its rival, in this case the human mind.

The difference is that humans are deeply and perpetually aware of the gap between their senses and recollections, intuitions and interpretations, maps and territories. The gap is the very vessel and condition, warp and womb of thought. The gap is the channel of interpretation between symbols and objects.

Denying the interpretant does not remove the gap. It remains intractably present. If the inexorable uncertainty, complexity, and information overflows of the gap are not consciously recognized and transcended, the gap fills up with noise. Congesting the gap are surreptitious assumptions, ideology, bias, manipulation, and static. AI triumphalism allows it to sink into a chaos of constantly changing but insidiously tacit interpretations.

Ultimately AI assumes a single interpretant created by machine learning as it processes ever more zettabytes of data and converges on a single interpretation. This interpretation is always of a rearview mirror. Artificial intelligence is based on an unfathomably complex and voluminous look at the past. But this look is always a compound of slightly wrong measurements, thus multiplying its errors through the cosmos. In the real world, by contrast, where interpretation is decentralized among many individual minds—each person interpreting each symbol—mistakes are limited, subject to ongoing checks and balances, rather than being inexorably perpetuated onward.

Reality does not gather in data centers or clouds; it is intrinsically distributed in human minds. The reach toward unity is essentially religious, as each human aspires toward a creator that he can never fully know. All humans must leap before they really look. Faith precedes knowledge.

5. Is "Quantum" the Answer?

WHENEVER PEOPLE POINT TO THE LIMITS OF AI, AI PROPHETS point to a transformative new computer invention on the horizon that will transcend all these perplexities. It is, they say, the quantum computer. Involving the manipulation of single molecules or miniscule superconducting loops, a quantum computer can theoretically perform analog computations that no Turing machine can simulate.

Expand the quantum computer to the data center with IBM, Google, and D-Wave, so the advocates of quantum computing promise, and artificial intelligence can attain powers far beyond the domains of human minds and deterministic logic. They believe that they can effect an astronomical speedup by changing the *bit* to the quantum bit, or *"qubit."*

The qubit is one of the most enigmatic tangles of matter and ghost in the entire armament of physics. Like a binary digit, it can register 0 or 1; what makes it quantum is that it can also register a nonbinary "superposition" of 0 and 1.

In 1989 I published a book, *Microcosm*, with the subtitle *The Quantum Era in Economics and Technology. Microcosm* made the observation that all computers are quantum machines in that they shun the mechanics of relays, cogs, and gears, and manipulate matter from the inside following quantum rules. But they translate all measurements and functions into rigorous binary logic—every bit is 1 or 0. At the time I was writing *Microcosm*, a few physicists were speculating about a computer that used qubits rather than bits, banishing this translation process and functioning directly in the quantum domain.

Quantum computers are acting in that domain, where current Turing machines fail. When the features of chips become small enough, the chip can no longer function as a determinist logical device. For example, today the key problem in microchips is to avoid spontaneous quantum tunneling, where electrons can find themselves on the other side of a barrier that by the laws of classical physics would have been insurmountable and impenetrable.

In digital memory chips or processors, spontaneous tunneling can mean leakage and loss. In a quantum computer, though, such quantum effects may endow a portfolio of features, providing a tool or computational "primitive" that enables simulation of a world governed by quantum rules.

One of the early voices calling for a quantum computer was Richard Feynman, in 1981 at a groundbreaking MIT "Physics of Computation" conference. Boolean machines, Feynman noted, cannot calculate the intricacies of entanglement, which is fundamental to all quantum behavior. For him, the point of a quantum computer would be to understand quantum mechanics better; but in the early nineties a series of breakthroughs suggested that entanglement would enable cryptographic and computing feats.

What is entanglement? A long-ago thought experiment of Einstein's showed that once any two photons—or other quantum entities—interact, they remain in each other's influence no matter how far they travel across the universe (as long as they do not interact with something else). Schrödinger christened this "entanglement": The spin—or other quantum attribute—of one behaves as if it reacts to what happens to the other, even when the two are impossibly remote.

In China in 2019, Pan Jianwei (working with Anton Zeilinger, his PhD advisor of a decade earlier in Vienna), demonstrated the long-distance entanglement of photonic messages between satellites 1,200 miles apart. Since any invasion of the link would destroy the entanglement, this mysterious quantum effect could assure the integrity of a connection. This would be true whether over great distances, or within the tiny gates of a quantum computer.

Interpretant/Observer

BEFORE ANYONE WAS TALKING of quantum computation, Turing ate his fatal poisoned apple, dying a few weeks before his forty-second birthday in 1954. But one of his projects in the last months of his life was an attempt to rethink quantum mechanics (this involved, he wrote in a postcard, "Hyperboloids of wondrous Light / Rolling for aye through Space and Time"). In this mental quantum play, he discovered something serious: continual observation or measurement will immobilize a quantum system. If you can "see" it, it isn't there.

Turing's observer paradox was (as his friend Robin Gandy reported) "pooh-poohed" by the physicists they talked with. But in the more receptive 1970s, it was rediscovered as the "quantum Zeno effect," tracing a well-trodden quantum path from dismissal to routine incarnation in the quantum optics laboratory.

Turing's paradox stems from the strange, unresolved, and seemingly unavoidable subjectivity of quantum mechanics. On the dissent, Einstein sardonically asked, "Do you really believe the moon exists only when you look at it?"[1] On the other side, John Wheeler provocatively spoke of "*it* from *bit*" and "the elementary act of observer-participancy": "in short... all things physical are information-theoretic in origin and this is a *participatory universe*."[2]

At a sufficiently small scale, Turing wrote, you are measuring atoms with atoms. Thus you incur the intrinsic uncertainty of self-referential loops. Most fundamental of all self-referential circularity, in Turing's view, is Heisenberg's explanation of his uncertainty principle, measuring atoms and electrons using instruments composed of atoms and electrons.

Like the uncertainty principle, like the *reductio-ad-absurdum* macroscopic qubit known as Schrödinger's cat, like the two-slit conundrum of infinite waves and definite particles, the enigma of the quantum observer reflects the most profound insights of mathematical logic.

The need for an observer in quantum mechanics repeats the need for an "interpretant" between object and symbol in Peirce's triadic logic, the need for external axioms in Gödel's incompleteness theorem, the need for a nonmechanistic "oracle" in Turing machines, and the need in general for logical schemes to avoid self-referential loops. It also incapacitates the quantum computer as a self-sufficient processor of deterministic AI algorithms.

Input/Output

WHATEVER THE EXPECTATIONS OF its advocates, quantum computing is an *analog* process. It shifts the burden from the internal "quantum" calculations to the front-end where the data is defined. Then it creates new perplexities at the back-end where the outputs are resolved.

With quantum computing, you still face the problem of creating an analog machine that does not accumulate errors as it processes its data. As long as it is analog, the process is virtually instantaneous, but we can't look in. Expand the process to the universe with Richard Feynman and MIT's Seth Lloyd, and you still face the input/output (I/O) problem: how you define meaningful outputs and solutions. The exercise resembles the invention of multiple parallel universes as a last-ditch solution to the problem of the observer in quantum mechanics.

Some proponents of quantum computing deem the entire universe an omniscient quantum computer that calculates everything instantly. But, once again, we see that like all analog computing, quantum processing shifts the burden of computation to input-output, preparation of the data and reading it.

Constrained by its input/output, the quantum machine increases processing speeds as long as the problem to be computed becomes more unbounded, less clearly defined. When the problem expands to the universe, everything is computed instantly. But amorphous answers impose a new challenge of interpretation. The Peirce triadic dilemma of symbols, objects, and interpretants remains. The focus becomes the framing of the questions or algorithms—essentially prayers—and reading the answers.

Physics departments everywhere benefit from the quantum computing campaign, which gives their students a newly relevant and fashionable
framework for their studies. But the temptation to treat this endeavor as
a national security grail, or even crisis, suggests why governments should
not control technology. They are too gullible and subject to fashions.

At best, the quantum computer is a special purpose analog device.
Less a technology than a series of stunts are the advances of Google
and its rivals parlaying seventy-two qubits and beyond into so-called
"quantum supremacy."

6. The Mind of a Mollusk

Hitting the energy wall and the lightspeed barrier, any chip's architecture will necessarily break up. It fragments into separate modules and asynchronous and more parallel structures. We might term these processors time-space "mollusks"—Einstein's word for entities in a relativistic world governed by the speed of light.

On chips, light speed translates to nine inches a nanosecond. Since a major processor chip can have as much as a thousand miles of infinitesimal wires, the nanoseconds add up. The resulting microcosmic distance of electron-nanoseconds is comparable to light years in the cosmos.

Governing the universal clock-pulse that regulates logic processing, step by step, across the chip, the lightspeed limit impels localization of functions. To reiterate: the space-time constraint will enforce a distribution of computing capabilities analogous to the distribution of human intelligence.

Forcing this distribution are the energy constraints of computation. Computers must now be measured not by the conventional metrics of operations per second, but by operations per watt. Regulating silicon is connectomic density and distance.

In operations per watt, the prevailing champion is made not of silicon but of carbon. It is the original neural network, the human brain and its fourteen watts, which is not enough to illuminate the incandescent light bulb over a character's head in a cartoon strip. In the future, computers will pursue the energy ergonomics of brains rather than the megawattage of Big Blue or even the giant air-conditioned expanses of data centers. All computers will have to use the power-saving techniques that have been developed in the battery-powered smartphone industry and then move on to explore the energy economics of real carbon brains.

For all the grandiose talk of AI usurping brains, this requirement to imitate them provides a humbling lesson. There is a critical difference between programmable machines and programmers. The machines are deterministic and the programmers are creative.

Robert Marks, of the Walter Bradley Center for Natural and Artificial Intelligence, explains the canonical example from biology:

> Biologists in the mid-twentieth century were excited by the advent of computers that could simulate evolution. Millions of generations could be simulated in a few seconds. But evolution simulation on a computer is algorithmic. It requires computer code. Creativity is non-algorithmic and therefore uncomputable...
>
> Design theorist William Dembski and I built on the *No Free Lunch* theorem, showing that the creative information added to an evolution program could be measured in bits. Computer simulations of popular evolutionary algorithms demonstrate that evolutionary programs need this active information. The programmer must contribute creativity to make the code work.[1]

So the AI movement, far from replacing human brains, is going to find itself imitating them. Just as the time-space constraint requires computers to break up into distributed and parallel functions, computer programs like artificial intelligence will have to respond to a mandate for modularity. The brain demonstrates the superiority of the edge over the core: It's not agglomerated in a few air-conditioned nodes but is dispersed far and wide, interconnected by myriad sensory and media channels.

The test of the new global ganglia of computers and cables, worldwide webs of glass and light and air, is how readily they take advantage of unexpected contributions from free human minds in all their creativity and diversity. These high-entropy phenomena cannot even be readily measured by the metrics of computer science.

(Even actual mollusks, without an integrated brain and without "infinite ink," command separate nervous systems unlinked to any cloud of concentrated intelligence.)

As the nanotech virtuoso James Tour of Rice University has demonstrated in his laboratory, graphene, carbon nanotube swirls, and other carbon compounds make possible an array of nanomachines, vehicles, and engines. They offer the still-remote promise of new computer architectures that can actually model physical reality as Feynman hoped. But they have nothing to do with minds, except the one that indispensably creates them.

7. GÖDEL VERSUS THE SINGULARITY

THE CURRENT GENERATION IN SILICON VALLEY MUST COME TO terms with the findings of von Neumann and Gödel early in the last century. Gödel's invention of a virtual computer architecture led to his incompleteness proof. Turing adopted the Gödel system and incorporated it in his Universal Computer model, which was based on oracles outside the system analogous to Gödel's unprovable axioms.

Once the current AI generation has absorbed Gödel and Turing, they must confront the breakthroughs in information theory of Claude Shannon, Gregory Chaitin, Anton Kolmogorov, and Shannon's colleague John R. Pierce. AI is a system built on the foundations of computer logic, and when Silicon Valley's AI theorists push the logic of their case to a "singularity," they defy the most crucial findings of twentieth-century mathematics and computer science.

For example, in a series of powerful arguments, Chaitin, the inventor of algorithmic information theory, has translated Gödel into modern terms. As I read Chaitin, all logical schemes are incomplete and depend on propositions that they cannot prove. Any logical or mathematical argument at its extremes—whether "renormalized" infinities or parallel universe multiplicities or imaginative superminds—starts falling off the cliffs of Gödelian incompleteness.

Chaitin's "mathematics of creativity" suggests that in order to push the technology forward it will be necessary to transcend the deterministic mathematical logic that pervades existing computers. Information theory depicts creativity as high-entropy, unexpected bits. Deterministic systems supply low-entropy carriers for creative activity. But creativity itself cannot be deterministic without prohibiting the very surprises that define information and reflect real creation. Gödel dictates a mathematics of creativity.

Unfortunately, you can read a hundred books on artificial intelligence and machine learning without encountering a single serious engagement of these showstoppers from the giants of computer science and information theory. Instead, the exponents of "strong" AI offer triumphalist analogies. Existing AI robots are deemed precursors of a robotic imperium, like a lily pond that begins nearly empty of lily pads and fills up in an exponential swoosh. Following the earlier coinage of Henry Adams describing nineteenth-century energy technologies, Kurzweil dubs AI progress a "Law of Accelerating Returns." At some point, the human epoch ends and an epoch of machine control ensues.

However, this fashionable singularity scenario depends on a set of little-understood assumptions common in the artificial intelligence movement:

- *The Modeling Assumption*: A computer can deterministically model a brain.
- *The Big Data Assumption*: The bigger the dataset, the better. No diminishing returns to big data.
- *The Binary Reality Assumption*: Reliable links exist between maps and territories, computational symbols, and their objects.
- *The Ergodicity Assumption*: In the world, the same inputs always produce the same outputs.
- *The Locality Assumption*: Actions of human agents reflect only immediate physical forces impinging directly on them.
- *The Digital Time Assumption*: Time is objective and measured by discrete increments.

For the game of Go, all these assumptions are essentially true. Go is deterministic and ergodic; any specific arrangement of stones will always produce the same results, according to the rules of the game. The stones are at once symbols and objects; they are always mutually congruent: the map *is* the territory. The effects of moves are immediate and local, according to the definitions and rules of the game. The overall system is determinist and Newtonian, governed by a single scheme of predetermined and unchangeable logic, and a single universal clock. The existing state of play is always the cumulative result of moves in the past.

Ergodicity is crucial to any predictive model. If the model itself generates a variety of outcomes, sure prediction is impossible. Unfortunately for prophets, the real world generates a huge multiplicity of outcomes from a tiny number of regularities.

But AI systems resemble a game of Go. AI assumes reality is determinist, capturable by big data, binary, ergodic, local, and orderly in time, with the future shaped by the cumulative moves of the past. AI assumes the objects in the universe are accurately rendered in the symbols in the machine. They assume no gap or necessary interpretant between symbols and objects. AI always works on an objective digital clock one step at a time. AI assumes congruence of maps and territories. The AI universe is discrete, digital, and monotonically encodable in the symbol system of the program.

Plausible on the Go board and other game arenas, these principles are absurd in real world situations. Symbols and objects are only roughly correlated. Diverging constantly are maps and territories, population statistics and crowds of people, climate data and the actual weather, the word and the thing, the idea and the act. Differences and errors add up as readily and relentlessly on gigahertz computers as lily pads on the famous exponential pond.

In order to have correspondence between logical systems and real world causes and effects, engineers have to interpret the symbols rigorously and control them punctiliously and continuously. Programmers have continually to enforce an interpretive scheme between symbols and objects that banishes all slippage. There can be no disproportionate "butterfly effects," black swans, entrepreneurial surprises, radical entropy, or novelty.

Big data from billions of sensors and sources does not begin to comply with any of these rules. The idea that machine learning in the real world can function like machine learning in AlphaGo is delusional.

The autonomous automobile is a good test case. The machine learner in your self-driving car cannot rely on the accuracy of the map that governs it. It cannot mistake the map for the territory. It cannot assume that the cumulative database from the past—its deterministic rearview mirror world—will hold in the future.

Instead your self-driving car must navigate a world that everywhere diverges from its maps, that undergoes combinatorial explosions of novelty, black swans fluttering up and butterfly effects flapping, that incurs tornadoes, blizzards and fogs, ice patches and potholes, that presents a phantasmagoria of tumbling tumbleweeds, plastic bags inflated by wind, inebriated human drivers making subjective projections and mistakes, pot-headed pedestrians and other high-entropy surprises.

Nonetheless, most "autonomy" companies base their plans on the six assumptions. Their self-driving cars depend on digital maps and their congruence with territories.

To achieve congruence, either you can change the cars or you can change the territories.

Most existing self-driving cars depend on changing the territories. They increasingly require the reconstruction of cities to accord with the maps of the designers. The Chinese, who lead the field, are in fact doing this—building entire systems to accommodate the cars, which in turn become new virtual railroads. This is a different goal than that envisaged by the singularitarians: vehicles independent of human guidance or control.

The map is a low-entropy carrier. The world is a flurry of high entropy and noisy messages, with its relevant information gauged by its degree of unexpectedness. To deal with the world, self-driving cars need to throw away the AI assumptions. They need to achieve faster and more sensitive four-dimensional vision systems rather than chasing the fool's errand of perfect maps.

As George Dyson, technology historian and philosopher, writes: "Complex networks—of molecules, people or ideas—constitute their own simplest behavioral descriptions. This behavior can be more accurately captured by continuous analog networks than by digital algorithmic codes."[1]

The best, most complex, and most subtle analog computer remains the human brain. AI poses no threat to it whatsoever.

8. AI's Promise

ARTIFICIAL INTELLIGENCE DOES OFFER HUGE PROMISE FOR MANKIND. Chinese technology titan and capitalist leader Ren Zhengfei, Huawei's prophetic founder, described some of the potential. Speaking to a Canadian reporter in May 2019, he projected a cornucopian future:

> We [at Huawei] can produce a premium phone from scratch in about 20 seconds, but very few staff work on our production lines.... The level of precision required for manufacturing the phones is 10 microns. People simply cannot do this. We must rely on machines... and image recognition [to achieve the necessary precision]. [On a larger scale], we can develop AI powered tractors which can work in the field 24/7 without needing to worry about mosquitoes, the cold, or storms... at a higher quality... and in remote areas where people will not go. This will create more wealth for humanity.
>
> With the help of AI, one person will be able to do the work that is done by 10 people today. This means that Canada would be equivalent to an industrial nation with 300 million people, Switzerland to an industrial nation with 80 million people, and Germany to an industrial nation with 800 million people.... In the future, a small group of people are very likely to generate huge amounts of wealth.[1]

In other words, Ren predicts a productivity explosion. But an explosion of productivity does not mean an evaporation of work. AI will make people more productive, and thus more employable. It will create new and safer and more interesting work. It will generate the capital to endow new companies and new ventures, as new technologies have done throughout history.

What it will not do is create a mind.

ENDNOTES

INTRODUCTION

1. David Silver et al., "Mastering the Game of Go Without Human Knowledge," *Nature* 550 (October 19, 2107): 354–359, https://doi.org/10.1038/nature24270.

2. Paul Werbos first described this process in his 1974 dissertation, which is included in his book *The Roots of Backpropagation: From Ordered Derivatives to Neural Networks and Political Forecasting* (New York: John Wiley & Sons, 1994). See also Paul Werbos, "Backpropagation Through Time: What It Does and How to Do It," *Proceedings of the IEEE* 78, no. 10 (October 1990): 1550–1560, https://doi.org/10.1109/5.58337.

3. D. B. Parker, "Learning Logic: Casting the Cortex of the Human Brain in Silicon," Technical Report Tr-47, Center for Computational Research in Economics and Management Science, MIT, Cambridge, MA.

4. David E. Rumelhart, Geoffrey E. Hinton, and Ronald J. Williams, "Learning Representations by Backpropagating Errors," *Nature* 323, no. 6088 (October 1986): 533–536, https://doi.org/10.1038/323533a0.

5. John Holland, *Adaption in Natural and Artificial Systems* (Cambridge, MA: MIT Press, 1975).

6. John Koza, *Genetic Programming: On the Programming of Computers by Means of Natural Selection* (Cambridge, MA: MIT Press, 1992).

7. Hassabis is quoted in an interview reported by Kyle Wiggers, "Open AI Launches Neural MMO, a Massive Reinforcement Learning Simulator," VentureBeat (website), March 4, 2019, https://web.archive.org/web/20190330110525/https://venturebeat.com/2019/03/04/openai-launches-neural-mmo-a-massive-reinforcement-learning-simulator/.

8. Kai-Fu Lee, *AI Superpowers: China, Silicon Valley, and the New World Order* (New York: Houghton Mifflin Harcourt, 2018).

9. "AlphaFold: Using AI for Scientific Discovery," DeepMind (website), January 15, 2020, https://web.archive.org/web/20200115182246/https://www.deepmind.com/blog/article/AlphaFold-Using-AI-for-scientific-discovery.

1. BEGINNINGS AT BLETCHLEY PARK

1. Irving John Good, "Speculations Concerning the First Intelligent Machine," *Advances in Computers*, vol. 6 (New York: Academic Press, 1965), 33, https://web.archive.org/web/20200924144953/https://exhibits.stanford.edu/feigenbaum/catalog/gz727rg3869.

2. Quoted in Jimmy Soni and Rob Goodman, *A Mind at Play: How Claude Shannon Invented the Information Age* (New York: Simon & Schuster, 2017), 216.

3. Elon Musk, Twitter, August 2, 2014, 9:33 p.m., https://twitter.com/elonmusk/status/495759307346952192.

4. Stephen Hawking, interview by Rory Cellan-Jones, BBC, video, 5:07, December 2, 2014, https://www.bbc.com/news/av/technology-30299992/stephen-hawking-full-interview-with-rory-cellan-jones.

5. Max Tegmark, *Life 3.0: Being Human in the Age of Artificial Intelligence* (New York: Knopf, 2017).

6. Alan Turing, "Systems of Logic Based on Ordinals" (PhD diss., Princeton University, 1938), 172–173. See The Turing Digital Archive, images 12 and 13, https://web.archive.org/web/20031007003245/http://www.turingarchive.org/browse.php/B/15.

2. RAPTURE OF THE NERDS?

1. Daniel Hillis, *The Pattern on the Stone* (New York: Basic Books, 1998).

2. W. Daniel Hillis, "The Connection Machine" (PhD diss., MIT, 1985), 10, https://web.archive.org/web/20200924151035/https://dspace.mit.edu/bitstream/handle/1721.1/14719/18524280-MIT.f?sequence=2.

3. Luiz André Barroso, Jimmy Clidaras, and Urs Hölzle, "The Datacenter as a Computer: An Introduction to the Design of Warehouse-Scale Machines," in *Synthesis Lectures on Computer Architecture Series*, ed. Mark D. Hill (San Rafael, CA: Morgan & Claypool, 2013), 47, https://web.archive.org/web/20200924151335/https://www2.cs.uic.edu/~brents/cs494-cdcs/papers/DC-Computer.pdf.

4. Frank Rosenblatt, quoted in Harding Mason, D. Stewart, and Brendan Gill, "Rival," *The New Yorker*, December 6, 1958.

5. One of Kurzweil's accounts of his conversation with Rosenblatt can be seen here, during a panel discussion moderated by David Kirkpatrick: "The Evolution Revolution," Techonomy (website), December 2, 2016, video and transcript, https://web.archive.org/web/20170723041244/https://techonomy.com/conf/te16/videos-artificial-intelligence/the-evolution-revolution/.

6. Ray Kurzweil, *How to Create a Mind: The Secret of Human Thought Revealed* (New York: Penguin, 2012).

7. Quoted in George Gilder, *The Silicone Eye* (New York: Norton & Company, 2005), 71.

3. TWO ZETTABYTE "CONNECTOMES"

1. Kevin Kelly, "Kevin Kelly," The Entertainment Gathering Blog, December 4, 2007, https://web.archive.org/web/20071208081626/https://blog.the-eg.com/2007/12/04/kevin-kelly/.

2. Personal conversation between Stretton and the author. A further summary of Stretton's work can be found at the University of Wisconsin–Madison's Department of Integrative Biology webpage: https://web.archive.org/web/20200728071019/https://integrativebiology.wisc.edu/staff/stretton-antony/. Likewise, Anthony Movshon of New York University says, "I think it's fair to say... that our understanding of the worm has not been materially enhanced by having that connectome available to us. We don't have a comprehensive model of how the worm's nervous system actually produces the behaviors. What we have is a sort of a bed on which we can build experiments—and many people have built many elegant experiments on that bed. But that connectome by itself has not explained anything." Quoted in Ferris Jabr, "The Connectome Debate: Is Mapping the Mind of a Worm Worth It?" Scientific American (October 2, 2012), https://www.scientificamerican.com/article/c-elegans-connectome/. See also "Can We Understand the Brain the Way We 'Understand' New York City?," Mind Matters News, Walter Bradley Center for Artificial Intelligence, March 4, 2020, https://web.archive.org/web/20200423161500/https://mindmatters.ai/2020/03/can-we-understand-the-brain-the-way-we-understand-new-york-city/.

3. Sebastian Seung, Connectome: How the Brain's Wiring Makes Us Who We Are (New York: Houghton Mifflin Harcourt, 2012), xvi.

5. Is "Quantum" the Answer?

1. Recounted in Abraham Pais, "Einstein and the Quantum Theory," Reviews of Modern Physics 51 (October 1, 1979): 907, https://doi.org/10.1103/RevModPhys.51.863.

2. John A. Wheeler, "Information, Physics, Quantum: The Search for Links," in Complexity, Entropy, and the Physics of Information, ed. Wojciech Hubert Zurek (Redwood City, CA: Addison-Wesley, 1990), 311. Emphasis in original.

6. The Mind of a Mollusk

1. Robert J. Marks, "What One Thing Do AI, Evolution, and Entrepreneurship All Need?," Mind Matters News, Walter Bradley Center for Artificial Intelligence, May 17, 2019, ce, May 17, 2019, https://web.archive.org/web/20200423164321/https://mindmatters.ai/2019/05/hat-one-thing-do-ai-evolution-and-entrepreneurship-all-need/.

7. Gödel versus the Singularity

1. George Dyson, Turing's Cathedral: The Origins of the Digital Universe (New York: Vintage Books, 2012), 280.

8. AI's Promise

1. Ren Zhengfei, interview by Lisa LaFlamme, CTV National News, March 13, 2019, https://www.ctvnews.ca/video?clipId=1636658&playlistId=1.4339046&binId=1.810401&playlistPageNum=1&binPageNum=1.

INDEX

Made in the USA
Coppell, TX
13 December 2021

68262228R10039